Fort Robinson Breakout

From Nowhere to Now Here

Michael Yanuck MD PhD

ISBN: 978-1-946600-34-9

DEDICATION

For Phillip Whiteman Jr., Marty Young Bear,
Dan Foster, my wife, my father,
and all the unnamed individuals of the Reservations
who took me into their hearts and minds
and made this work possible.

.

Names of people and places have been changed, and most of the characters presented here represent composites of more than one person, and, in some cases, happenings pertaining to one person are ascribed to another. Although not always presented in the order they occurred, the events of this story are otherwise based on real events.

Little Wolf had gone to the agent about the middle of the summer and said to him: "This is not a good country for us, and we wish to return to our home in the mountains where we were always well. If you have not the power to give permission, let some of us go to Washington and tell them there how it is, or do you write to Washington and get permission for us to go back."

"Stay one more year," replied the agent, "and then we will see what we can do for you." "No," said Little Wolf. "Before another year there will be none left to travel north. We must go now."

~Charles A. Eastman, Indian Heroes and Great Chieftains

CHAPTER ONE

In the dead of night April and I followed a bus carrying Reservation children to a place called "The Last Hole," where many of their ancestors had been annihilated after breaking free from their captivity at Fort Robinson more than a century ago.

As the children stood silent, Frank Lightning paced the hallowed ground, then struck a solemn tone.

"After they were killed," he told them, "their bodies were shipped to the Smithsonian, so that they could be analyzed for the effects of gunpowder shot at close range. They weren't even given a decent burial. They weren't treated like human beings. Just subjects to be studied. It took a hundred years of requisitioning the government before their body parts were released. We brought them here, and then to Busby to show them that their sacrifice hadn't been in vain, but because of them, their people had a homeland."

"That's why we make this run," he declared. "Because we're not 'dog eaters' – We're 'spirit seekers' – We're fierce warriors on a spiritual journey about the life and preservation of our traditions and our people…"

CHAPTER TWO

After a brief ceremony in which he burned sage and sprinkled cedar and offered prayers at the site, Frank led the children back on the bus.

On the return drive to Fort Robinson, I looked at April, concerned how she might be reacting to all this? Whether it was disturbing to her and bringing back unwanted memories about how her family had been mostly murdered by the Nazis during the Holocaust?

"No," she answered.

She hesitated and collected her thoughts.

"It was weird," she continued. "I had never visited the killing fields of Poland and other places. And I always tried to avoid the thought of the Holocaust and never liked it when you would talk to people and write these stories about the Holocaust that you were so interested in it. It was just something I never wanted to think about. What's the point? It's like my grandmother said, 'There was nothing there but blood.'

"But here, it was actually healing. Because I was praying with these friends of yours, who represent this other nation, this other people, who have been massacred. And in a strange way it became healing to me. It became a substitute of the killing fields of my family..."

CHAPTER THREE

Arriving back at the Fort, April and I followed Frank and the children into the auditorium. Inside, Frank pulled me aside.

"I want you to talk to the runners," he said. "Tell them about your experiences on the Reservations where you've been."

I shook my head.

"Frank, I don't think I can do this," I said. "We just got back from a place where their descendants were murdered and then studied. I'm a student of your ways. I shouldn't be lecturing anyone."

"No, they'll understand," he insisted. "Because you want to help them, and to help preserve their ways…"

I stood before the gathering.

"I appreciate your warm reception," I said. "Frank asked me to talk about my experience on the Reservation where I'm working. Before I start, maybe I'll tell you a little about myself and how I got to the Reservation.

"Most of my life I wanted to be a cancer scientist. My grandfather had died of cancer when I was young, and since then, I wanted to do something to help cure that disease. While a medical student, I was accepted for a scholarship to work at the National Institutes of Health, and worked in a lab to develop a vaccine for cancer. I had just worked out a vaccine for cancer that had been approved for clinical trials in terminal cancer patients by the FDA. I was on my way to achieving my life's goal.

"Then, I suffered a leg injury. For a year I dragged my leg around. I was in constant pain, and the problem just got was worse, no matter what treatment I received. In fact, the medications just made me worse and caused significant side effects, like stomach upset and ulcer.

"Finally, my doctors told me that I wasn't going to get better, and I could expect chronic pain, and wouldn't walk normally, and I just had to accept that.

"Well, before that, if anyone had ever told me to try other forms of medicine, I would have told them, 'No way,' and sneered at anything that was outside of the mainstream. I would have never considered 'Oriental medicine' – No one was going to insert a needle into me - nor Osteopathic approaches - I had no interest in being 'popped.'

"But it felt like everything had been taken away and I wasn't being offered any other choices, so I went down that 'alternative' road.

"And – long story short – it led me in the direction of a certain way of life. One based on service to those in greatest need and an openness to more ways of healing than just those taught in medical school.

"The years passed, and one thing led to another, so that I found myself on a Reservation. And not long after I visited the Reservation for the first time, there was a rash of suicides. On the Memorial Day weekend, I think about six young people took their lives.

"I was stunned, and sought ways to prevent this kind of occurrence in the future. I talked to community leaders, and found that they were also searching for ways to help and heal.

"They brought in Frank, as well as other traditional healers who practiced Native American ceremonies; and I was surprised to learn that many of these approaches were similar to the ones that helped me.

"Now, my concern is that many of your healing practices are being lost. With the death of elders, with the loss of indigenous languages and practices and customs, I think there is the potential for these practices to be lost as well. I'd like to see them preserved, not just for what they have to give to the native community, but for the benefit of all people..."

CHAPTER FOUR

Handing the microphone back to Frank, he addressed the children.

"I hope you all heard what Dr. Mike had to say," he said. "He's talking about the preservation of your traditions, and why it's important, and the dysfunction that exists on the Reservations, and how it's in our own culture to overcome that dysfunctional behavior, and return to being a strong people."

Frank gave me back the microphone.

"A short time after learning about the suicides on the Reservation," I offered, reticently, "I was talking to a local restaurant owner. He'd established a restaurant where all the money generated goes to the Lakota Youth Center – 'To the healing of our children,' he said. 'So that they can know their traditions, and grow up to be strong.' He told me, 'Our way teaches us that the problem isn't in falling down, the problem is not getting up again – because then you haven't acquired that strength that you were meant to. Most of our old ways have been lost or let go or forgotten - mostly because of the historical trauma that our people have been through. But, if we want, we can still embrace those ways. And I'd like to see that our young people have that choice.'

"And listening, I thought, 'Given the collective hurts that the people here had sustained, this could become a community of the strongest individuals in the world.'"

At that moment, the children erupted in spontaneous applause, and, without any prompting, formed a line and one-by-one approached me to shake my hand...

CHAPTER FIVE

Just before initiating the Breakout Run, all were offered war paint applied to their faces.

I declined, saying I didn't want to take away from what the kids were going to do, and it was for them to carry on this legacy.

Then, I noticed April had had war paint applied.

"It's like Frank said," she responded. "It's about being a 'spiritual warrior'."

I thought she looked as she had in the picture of her on the tree when she wore Indian garb and looked strong and defiant...

We accompanied the children to a jail cell that held their ancestors, after having been captured while trying to return to their ancestral homeland. Then, at the appointed hour, they hurriedly broke free from the cell...

CHAPTER SIX

I looked on with another non-native person, who was there supporting the Breakout Run.

"I think it's important for any minority group, particularly for American Indians, not to lose that information that isn't written down someplace," he said. "It can only get passed down from elders to the kids – and kids do it with their kids. Particularly, when there's so much tradition is there is with American Indians, in the amount of suffering that they went through and being tossed around.

"I see what goes on here with the Pauite tribes in Nevada. Some of the tribal reservations are not too bad. But a lot of them are so run down that it's really not pretty. And then you have an Indian complex on the east side of town that was the first big school for native American kids that was started way back in the 1800's. and it's still being used more as a museum and historic location. It's boarded up now, and it would be a shame if that stuff gets lost.

"I was reading something in the war street journal about a guy from a cult who was teaching these American Indians their language because none of them could speak it anymore, and he had learned how to do it, so he had become the noted authority on their language for their Nation – and it was only because he'd been interested and spent so many years teaching himself, and the kids themselves had moved away from it. He's still having problems teaching it to the native kids, because if they can't text it, they don't want to deal with it anymore..."

CHAPTER SEVEN

Taking turns running for miles, the children followed the route that their ancestors had taken over a century ago. The land was mostly barren, so that children were mostly alone.

Then, banners were strewn along the roads welcoming the Fort Robinson Breakout runners as we entered the of the Pine Ridge Reservation.

At Wounded Knee the runners were met with excited cheers along their route and then greeted by the tribal President, members of the tribal council, as they were led inside a crowded auditorium filled to capacity with enthusiastic well-wishers.

"The Lakota of Pine Ridge have always had a feeling of trust and friendship with our relatives, the Cheyenne," the Tribal President said. "After the breakout in 1879, the members of this community nursed the survivors back to health. For several years, we hid them from the authorities in our Reservations before they returned to their homeland. We were like the outer circle of buffalo, putting them in the center of our community, with every person in the Tribe on the periphery looking out for them and protecting them from Calvary that was trying to flush them out and hunt them down..."

CHAPTER EIGHT

At the conclusion of Pine Ridge welcoming ceremony, we were invited to partake in a communal meal. As I sat partaking in the meal on the bleachers, one of the event's organizers, Marty, turned to me.

"So, Dr. Mike, did you find it hard to be a doctor on the Reservation?" he asked.

'Challenging' was the term I thought more appropriate of my time with the Indian Health Service (IHS). I suppose there are 'hard' parts to it. Not enough staff. Not enough supports. Not enough funding. But, in general, I felt as though I had the support of those I was caring for. They got me through the hard parts. Even for the most difficult patients, I felt as though they took me into their hearts and kept me going.

Marty smiled.

"That piece right there is what let you take your energy and redirect it, so that it could help you and the person who you were taking care of," he said. "Most people want to fight rather than take an attack on their ego. Whereas if you able to go more spiritual, then it will let those things help you.

"When I look at people and see them talking, 'That was ours,' and, 'This is ours,' that's ego. Whereas, if you're spiritual, you know that there's a whole life in a generation, and you don't have to hold on to things at all – you can let them go.

"And that's what our spirituality teaches us about science. We're all just atoms floating around here. That's why you can't possess things – because everything has its own energy and its own matter. If you can recognize that, you can let go of your ego, and overcome things. Whereas, if you don't, you just wind up holding on, until it finally kills you."

I told him about a conversation I'd had with Dr. Curtiz years before.

"He felt that because the Native American culture was all inclusive and it was coming up against a culture that was all exclusive – like Western Christianity – the exclusive culture would win out because it would insist on domination," I said.

"That's exactly what power versus force is about," he said. "The exclusive culture being one of force and taking over things, whereas, if you understand power, that power is able to absorb force and overcome it.

"So that's what's in Indian's DNA. To know about power. That's why were more accepting, and in our traditions, they taught us not to use force.

"Since we've been institutionalized, we've forgot that. Now, we have to put our kids back in a mindset to accept power and that there's an order in that power structure.

"There is an order in the force structure; but whereas you have to use force to overpower the circle, if you try to do that, the circle is just going to absorb that, and turn it around, and send it back out.

"Like if you look at someone who hates you, and you recognize that there is love in them, you'll make that love grow by recognizing it, and sending energy to it, and it will change their energy.

"So whereas there's someone out there using anger as a force, and you're aware of what they're doing, and you're also aware that they have love in them, and you're aware of it in yourself, and your aware of how it makes you feel, and recognize that, then that's going to grow in them, too, and actually change somebody's energy..."

CHAPTER NINE

I asked Marty what he meant by his earlier statement of taking something like "an attack on my ego," and why he didn't refer to it as trauma?

"For example, I think that I was traumatized by my father being overbearing," I said. "I don't regard it as an attack on my ego."

"I guess that it has to do with your recognition of force," he said. "What he was doing was using force by trying to control people. It was hurting you.

"But if you recognize it as a learning experience and that you had to go through it so that you could recognize it elsewhere - so that your father focused your energy in order to recognize it elsewhere, so that when you got there, you'd be able to help.

"So, if you look at it that way, then everybody here can be a teacher in some way. You have to be willing to learn and grow from that knowledge, and recognize that everybody out there is there to teach you.

"That's where healing comes from – by acknowledging it and finding the right frequency to counter that force.

"So whenever we see something that's out of balance out there, we recognize it due to our connection with the earth, and if we don't feel that connection, then we're not healthy, and we need to get back to our spiritual understandings.

"There's a spiritual understanding to every problem. Every problem that you see out that's ego driven is fixable by an understanding of your spiritual energy that's just the other side of the coin, but you don't go there because it's the hardest emotion to fix.

"I would rather be ready for enlightenment, and ready and secure in thinking about it, and then these kids over here will absorb that.

"It makes me feel good that I'm healthy and feel balanced, and they're going to think about it, and not be easily swayed by the dangers that are out there.

"Once you get connected to the divine power, people gravitate to you, like Jesus, or Buddha, or Crazy Horse. They say that just being in their presence was a miracle and worth being killed..."

CHAPTER TEN

Frank addressed those at the Tribal reception.

"The Indian way," he said, "is to put the elders and the children first, the women second, the braves and warriors after that, and the leaders come last. A leader in Indian society has to put his concerns at the bottom – because he needs to be thinking about his people first.

"The problem with the dominant culture is that it's the sickest that get ahead. It's the sickest that make the most money. It's the sickest that have the best jobs.

"Because in the dominant culture, it's the person with the best defense mechanisms that is rewarded. If you put others ahead – if you're sensitive – if you think about others first – you're going to come in last..."

CHAPTER ELEVEN

There were three older native women standing near me. Frank introduced them as the granddaughters of Chief Red Cloud. They told me that when it came to the boarding schools it has been the intention of their grandfather to send the young leaders for an education.

"My grandfather told them," said the eldest, "'You're going into the enemy's camp, to learn the enemy's ways, so to better be able to protect your people...'"

Afterwards, Frank pulled me aside.

"Indian grandma's lead the Indian nation," Frank joked. "Grandma told you to do something, you be shivering in your shoes if you didn't. Grandma will scold you, and she got the power..."

CHAPTER TWELVE

Frank indicated he'd been invited to talk at a University that was along the way.

"The native students have a high dropout rate there," he said. "They don't feel like they're connecting with their instructors, so they leave the university, and go back to the Reservation. The university has invited us to speak to see if we can offer them ideas on how to reach the students and something different that they can do..."

Arriving on the campus, Frank joked as we ascended the many rows of steps leading to the shiny, ivory University building where it had been arranged for him to speak.

"We are now taking the steps towards higher education," he said. "You know, I never finished high school, but I still acquired a BA. You know what that stands for?... 'Bad Attitude.'"

But within the packed auditorium, the mood he projected was quite different.

"Once there was a man in Europe who thought that his people were the best, and his culture was the best, and they needed more room to live," he began. "As a result, millions and millions of people were killed. And he provided the world with an example of the worst that could happen when you don't accept others – when you don't accept diversity.

"During that war, a lot of my people died jumping off of boats and fighting for this country. When Ira Hayes [the Native American and an American Marine who was one of the six men immortalized in the iconic photograph of the flag raising on Iwo Jima during World War II] lifted that flag, he was doing it for this country.

"Before going into battle, they would sing 'The Flag Song.' It's the equivalent to our national anthem. The words go like this, 'When you go across the water to defend your country, your land – when you raise that flag and as it waves, you earn that spirit of a warrior.' My daughter is fighting in Afghanistan now. She still sings that song. And I sing it when I pray for her.

"And at the Battle of the Little Big Horn, where some of my relatives died, they sang the Flag song. And then at Wounded Knee and at Washita and at Fort Robinson, where my ancestors were slaughtered for a way of life that they believed in."

"The Creator shows his love for diversity in His creations," he continued. "In the animals and plants and their diversity of life. Even mankind is all black, red, yellow and white – the four core colors of mother earth. The diverse colors that reflect in the rainbow – the vision of hope. Even through the many different languages. If you close your eyes and listen to those birds and prairie dogs and leaves. They say that our Cheyenne language comes right from the water, right from the earth, right from the trees and animals. When I speak in my language and offer prayer for guidance, you should be able to hear the sounds of all living things.

"My first language is Cheyenne. I was not introduced to English until I went to school. And it was difficult for me to learn English because it was so different. In my language – the Cheyenne language – it's very direct. We don't have conjunctions. There no 'and, but and or.' But then, when I studied the bible, I found that there, too, they had direct language. In the Ten Commandments, it says, 'Thou shall not kill.' 'Thou shall not steal.' It doesn't say, 'Thou shall not kill, except if it means the killing of Indians.' It doesn't say there, 'Thou shall not steal, except if it's a matter of manifest destiny and taking away Indian's land.'

"I'm not kidding about that. For a Cheyenne to be recognized as a human being, they had to go to court. And the only reason that they went to court over it was because they wanted to hang a group of Cheyenne, but they wouldn't let them because you could only execute a human being, and up until that time Cheyennes weren't seen as human. We were regarded as savages before that. Not even human.

"I come here because I'm looking for others who are searching for common ground. Who are spirit seekers and are looking to heal. And who are looking to promote healing – for us and for themselves..."

CHAPTER THIRTEEN

"Dr. Mike, there's a University professor here who wants to talk to me about my work with the kids," Frank said. "He invited me to his house. Would you and April like to go with me?..."

We arrived at the Professor's home after dark. Looking up at the patio on the second level, I was taken by the natural setting created by the cascading tree branches that in the front and back of the house.

The professor's wife greeted us at the door and showed us inside. It appeared that they were having a party and there were already a number of guests inside.

The professor was sitting at the table.

"How do you do?" he said.

The Professor inquired how we'd met Frank, and I responded by telling him about the Memorial Day suicide cluster. He nodded and listened, though seemed rather aloof as I described my experiences in the suicide prevention programs.

Frank, however, was his usual animated self.

"With most white people, I feel really dumb," Frank said. "I went through school failing everything. But when I'm with Dr. Mike, I feel really smart, because I can see the connections."

The professor asked Frank about his work with native children?

"Is there anything you do that has demonstrated results?" he asked.

"Mostly, I do workshops to demonstrate to people the problems of historical trauma," Frank responded. "If you want, we can do an exercise here with the people you have in your house."

The professor nodded and Frank called to those in the house.

"Com'on, everyone," Frank said. "We're going to do an exercise to demonstrate the kind of work I'm doing with Indian kids."

The group collected all along the walls of the living room.

"In the native culture, everything is centered on the next generation," Frank said. "To us, children are sacred. So, we have the child in the center, and he or she is brought up by an expanding circle of parents, and aunts and uncles, and then elders, and around them are the warriors, whose mission is to protect and provide for them."

"Now, who wants to be the child?" Frank asked.

Frank selected the Professor's young daughter for this role.

"Professor, you and the missus will be the parents," Frank continued. "Dr. Mike and Rachel, you be the aunt and uncle..."

Frank continued to select among those in the room to be the expanding group of relatives, then protectors, then elders.

"Now, what happens when I take away the child," Frank said, as he led the little girl to another room. "I've sent her away to boarding school, far away from all of you. How do you feel now?"

"Lonely," one woman said.

"Like I'm lacking a purpose," said another.

"Uh-huh," Frank said. He went into the other room and led the professor's daughter back into the room. "Now, twelve years later I bring the child back. But now the child isn't sure about rejoining the circle because she no longer knows how to speak her native language, and she doesn't know if she wants to anymore, because where she's been, she's been taught that her people are savages and their way is savage. She was beaten with a strap for speaking her language. Every night she cried and then she laid awake and thought, 'If I ever get married and have children, I'll never teach my children the language or all the Indian things that I know. I'll never teach them that, I don't want my children to be treated like they treated me.'"

Frank turned to another woman.

"How does that make you feel?" he asked.

The woman looked about, perplexed.

"It feels like gridlock," she said. "Like neither side knows how to react."

Frank turned to another woman.

"How about you?" he said.

"I feel sad," the woman said. "I feel like I have to respect the child's experience. It's as though the situation's hopeless, because I didn't know how to bring her back into the fold."

18

"Okay," Frank said, "what if I set down this medicine bundle in the center and tell you that it contains the lost ways of her people and that it has knowledge to help the child re-learn her peoples' ways and re-introduce her to her people again? What will you do then?"

And at that moment, Marty spontaneously stepped forward and took the medicine bundle with one hand and the girl with the other, then brought the girl back into the center.

And like a chain reaction rising from some spirit of hope, the rest of us spontaneously lifted our hands and locked arms and pulled each other into a tight-knit circle again...

CHAPTER FOURTEEN

At the completion of the exercise, Frank turned to the Professor, smiling.

"So, what do you think?" Frank asked.

"I don't think anything," responded the Professor.

"Oh, well, what do you feel?" Frank asked.

"Hmm, I don't feel anything either," the Professor replied.

"Well, what is your ethnic background?" asked Frank. "What culture do you come from?"

"I come from the Jewish culture," he said.

Then he addressed me.

"And it looks like you might come from the Jewish culture, too," he added.

Yes, I said.

"Do you belong to a Temple where you are?" he asked.

I hadn't really looked for one, I responded.

"Mike isn't religious," April inserted. "Ever since he visited the Reservation that first time, I tell other Jewish couples who ask, 'Mike's Jewish because his family is Jewish – really, he's a practicing Lakota.'"

She laughed.

"But just before we got married, I talked with Mike's uncle," she continued. "He told me that the family actually descended from the tribe Cohen and were 'The Keepers of the Light in the Temple.'"

"Yes, I happen to be a Cohen, too," the professor said.

Then, he turned to Frank.

"That means that we can trace our roots back some 3200 years to the time of Moses," he explained. "We are descendants of Mose's brother, Aaron, and come from a long line of Priests."

"Oh," said Frank. "Because I can trace my roots back to Chief Sweet Medicine, the Cheyenne prophet who told of the coming of the white man to this continent four generations before it happened."

April said that she was finding a lot of connections between the Jewish religion and Native American culture.

"Mike and I were unprepared for the long hike that was the 'Welcoming Back of the Thunder Being' ceremony. It was a long, strenuous, arduous and potentially dangerous ascent in the snow to the highest place on the Black Hills – called 'Harney's Point' – the highest place East of the Rockies on this continent and west of the Pyrenees in Europe! And yet the people making this climb were men and women, young children and elders alike - even babies. Because you're walking up as a nation - together."

"Jews before the destruction of the Temple," April added, "used to walk – not ride – to the temple and bring offerings. From the Galeel - or the Negev - all the way to Jerusalem, which is a high place. It might be a couple of days walk, carrying with you the fruit on your head, and the animals for the burnt offering to the Temple.

"Currently, the way Judaism is taught is intellectual. It tests the intellect. It's about remembering all these rules and all these stories – writing it down, arguing, thinking. It's very intellectual. Whereas the current way that the Native American religion is practiced right now, it's challenging the soul through challenging the body.

"It's like a lot of Jewish stuff is about challenging the mind, and, thereby, involving soul through the mind. It's like the vehicle for understanding the soul is the mind, whereas for Native Americans a lot of it is through the body."

"Yes, but there are those experiential aspects of the Jewish culture," the professor said. "And if you did participate in the four days of fasting, then you're more in tune with the mystic aspects of Judaism."

"Either way, it's okay," she responded. "People have different ways to understand the soul."

"You seem to know a lot about Indian culture," the professor said. "Do you have a special interest in it?"

"Well, even when I was growing up in Israel, I'd always been fascinated with Native cultures," she said. "After I graduated with my Art Conservator degree, my first job was with the National Museum of the American Indian. While I was there, I had a Native American boyfriend. He would always be asking me to visit his family in the Pueblo of Acoma near Albuquerque, but I never got there."

She smiled.

"Just before I came here," she said, "I was sitting down to dinner with my family and telling them that I was coming out here to visit Mike. So, my sister turns to me and says, 'Don't you think it's kind of funny that even with all the years you went out with this Native American guy, it took marrying a Jewish doctor to get you to an Indian Reservation?'"

She and the Professor laughed.

He asked which Reservation I worked on? I responded that until a week ago I'd been working at IHS Headquarters, but felt that I wasn't accomplishing anything aside from being attacked, so I'd accepted a position with the VA.

He bowed his head.

"Oh, I'm sorry," he said. "I'm sorry things turned out that way..."

CHAPTER FIFTEEN

Leaving the house, the Professor shook our hands and thanked us for coming.

"Enjoy the rest of your adventure," the Professor said.

As we walked to the car April asked what I thought of the interaction with the professor? I said that I'd been rather disappointed.

"Here's a man who interacts with native students on a daily basis," I said, "and he showed no ability to empathize - think or feel – in the exercise that Frank shared with him."

"Well, Mike, it's about baby steps," April said. "That's what it's all about. If you're going to be judgmental, then people are just going to close down – like what these Native American students are doing. They're probably with these professors who don't understand their culture, and as a result they're closing down and failing in their classes. And that's why you've been brought here – to help these instructors to understand their Native Americans students and show them how Native Americans are thinking and feeling – so that maybe they won't close down and they will make the effort to reach their students and help their students do better in their classes."

We got in the car.

"Mike, what do you think is your soul channel?" she asked.

I looked at her confused.

'Soul channel'? I repeated.

"Yes," she said. "Before we came here, I went to a seminar at a Seminary. According to the speaker, there are three different channels to work on your soul. One is knowledge and wisdom – learning. In Judaism that translates to studying Torah. The second is worship – prayer. The third one is doing things – the making of

23

good deeds. If you had to plug yourself in to one of these three, which would it be?"

Doing good deeds, I said. If you're not engaged in doing good, then there's no purpose to prayer or study.

She nodded.

"In so many ways," she said, "what's driving you is your father's voice in your head, saying, 'Well, what is it good for? What are you going to do with it?' It's all about work."

"But I think that you're on a spiritual path," she asserted.

"Do you understand the word 'cavana'?" she asked. "In Hebrew, it means, 'intention.' Your intention in going into primary care has always been to minister to the sick and those who have the hardest time accessing care. I think you came into your subspecialty with a cavana of working on your soul - with an intention of working on your soul. And I don't think everybody who is an Internal Medicine doc does that. Some of them do. But probably a lot go into it like, 'This is a job that can make me pretty good money.'"

She looked away.

"It's wrong what Headquarters did to you," she said. "But now I think you're going back to what you were meant to – with a focus of doing good deeds. You'll be working really hard, providing basic care to people who couldn't afford it or access it any other way."

"Lately, I have been thinking about these things," she continued. "I think my pillar is prayer. My way is chanting, or even making my art is my prayer. During the seminar, they said a good way to live your life is to live it like you're constantly giving back to God. And just being aware that God is around, and to always be thinking about that, and that the reason that we're here is to be working on our soul, and growing and making our soul better.

"And it makes me really happy that you share that kind of outlook on life. I don't think that it's easy to find another person who thinks that way, and I think that I'm growing into it while you already were there. When we first met, maybe I was thinking about that in a certain way, but not as crystallized as I think about that now.

"And if I would have gone into a relationship with somebody who wasn't thinking like that, it would have been hard. But instead, I'm growing into the way that you think, so it makes it easier to grow into that."

"So that's lucky for me," she concluded...

CHAPTER SIXTEEN

Arriving at our lodgings, Marty was quick to greet us.

"Frank said you worked in research," he commented. "He said you developed a cancer vaccine."

Yes, I said. The vaccine targeted mutations in a particular gene called p53, which is mutated in a majority of cancers.

"What's p53?" he asked.

The p53 gene was the gene responsible for suicide pathways within the cell; in cell that has normal p53, the p53 will trigger it to self-destruct when the cell is mutated. If the p53 is mutated, then the cell loses that ability.

April had been listening.

"How does a cell self-destruct?" she asked. "And why do the cancer cells not self- destruct?"

"When p53 detects problems in the cell – mutations – it orchestrates the cell suicide pathways that lead to that cell's self-destruction," I said. "but if you mutate the p53 gene, not only do you lose its self-destruct ability, but you can actually activate its ability to contribute to the transformation potential of cell and growth and malignant development."

"How do p53 mutation happen in cells?" she asked

In general, mutations are caused my free radicals generated by the carcinogens in cigarette smoke, or ultraviolet radiation from sunlight.

"They cause breaks in the DNA strand," I said. "Or else changes in the molecular structure of the building blocks in the DNA."

"That seems to imply an external source for the mutation," she said. "So how would a cell internally get rid of that mutation?"

The cells did have the ability to recognize changes.

"There are mechanisms within to repair the cell," I said.

"Does the p53 gene orchestrate the only mechanism for cell suicide?" she asked. "Or is there another mechanism?"

There were other mechanisms, I said.

"And are there mechanisms that can watch out for the p53 gene?" she asked. "And when it has damage, go and fix the damage, or else self-destruct when it senses damage to the p53 gene? Does the cell have that oversight and checks and balances? Does your T cell – the ones that you've generated with your vaccine – activate one of those checks and balances?... Why didn't that mechanism become active on its own?"

There could be many reasons, I said.

"Studies of AIDS shows us that in people whose immune system doesn't work properly, all kinds of spontaneous cancers develop," I said. "It's shown us that a healthy immune system is looking for cancers all the time in the body – a process called immune surveillance. And it could well be that its recognizing things like my p53 mutations and knocking them out in most people.

"But, in other people, maybe the immune system isn't as active, or isn't able to find the cancer cells, or maybe the cancer cells in those people have disguised the p53 mutation so it's harder to see."

"That's why I'm curious," April said. "A virus goes into a cell, and then uses it to make more of itself, so it makes sense that it would develop ways to evade the immune system.

"But a cancer cell – you wouldn't think would do that. Except that a lot of cancers are caused by viruses."

That was true. Like in the case of HPV and cervical cancer, which would effectively deactivated p53 and lead it to act as though it were mutated.

"Once you've done that, the cell wants to live despite its ill and abnormal state," I said. "It loosens the grip on the normal self-repair processes within the cell, so that mutations are ongoing. Effectively, the train just goes off the track when you knocked out something like p53. You can't maintain the kind of normal controls and differentiation that were once there."

"So, it's like genetic drift?" she asked.

Yes. In genetic drift, chromosomes duplicate themselves, and more and more mutations occur. And by doing these things, the cells find greater ways to live as individual entities within the body. It becomes like an invader – it grows and spreads and finds ways to evade the immune system.

"So in a sense a cancer cell becomes a rebel and an enemy," she said. "Is it a harder enemy to fight because it feels and looks so friendly?"

Yes, it most ways, it looks just like any other cell. It leaves the immune system to ponder the question, 'How do I fight myself?'

"So, it's almost like civil war," April said.

'Civil war'? I thought. I suppose that was fair to say, as for most cancers, the person had brought it upon him or herself.

"The initial insult is usually because of something that you knew better than doing," I said. "Whether it was smoking or sun exposure. The body is usually telling you. In most people who wind up with skin cancer, the body was giving them sunburns. It was telling them, 'Don't go out in that sun. You're hurting me. You're hurting yourself.'"

"So, it was like you had cancer cells that had forgotten how to self-destruct when they were doing harm to the body," Marty said, "because of the mutations that had happened in those cells because of toxic exposure. And the T-cells were reminding the cancer cell how to self-destruct."

"It's almost like the cancer cells are rebels without a cause," April said.

I couldn't bring myself to agree this time.

"What is their cause?" she asked.

Well, when somebody takes a drag on a cigarette, they expose their lung cells to carcinogens that can lead to mutations and the development of cancer. Most of these cells – like good soldiers – self-destruct rather than go on to become cancerous.

But the ones that don't – that escape this fate – are saying to the person – their host – "Hey, I've had enough of this! You're just trying to kill yourself! Why should I die for you? I'm going to find a way to keep on living."

April thought.

"But what about skin cancer and light?" she asked.

"You're exposing yourself to too much UV radiation," I said, "which in turn is activating mutations in the skin cells. It's the same carcinogenic process as with the cigarette. Mutations happen until the cells become cancerous. It's like they're saying, 'I'm not going to die anymore for you. I'm going to wait until you activate a mutation in the p53 molecule and I don't have to die anymore.'"

"You think that individual cells in the body have that sense?" she asked.

"They certainly have that ability," I responded. "We evolved from single-celled organisms. Every cell in the body comes from that ancestry. You might say that when a cell 'rebels,' it has essentially tapped into an earlier memory of being a single celled organism with a will to live."

"But that's it," Marty said. "Everything was put out of balance. The person is smoking or eating unhealthy things, and the body is reacting to it."

"But it's a dysfunctional reaction," he continued. "It's not the way that it's supposed to be. That's why you have to find a way to put things back in harmony again."

"Because they're going to die, too," April inserted. "Because they're killing the organism that's been feeding them. By extending their lives, they're killing the thing that's keeping them alive. So, it's still a death sentence. And where you're causing the person to die, you're not really helping matters. 'Rebels without a cause.'"

"Maybe, it's like you said," she concluded. "Anger. Empty, ancient cellular anger. But it's not going to result in anything good..."

CHAPTER SEVENTEEN

Our next stop was in a barren stretch of Reservation land, plagued with potholes on the roads and harsh winds and rain storms.

Frank asked me to join him for a healing circle involving some of the older members of the Tribe...

"Many of us are stuck in feelings of anger and depression," a female elder said, "and despair over how our people have been treated."

When I asked about the source of these hard feelings, the woman pointed in the direction of the swollen waterways.

"You're looking at it," the woman said. "The dam took away our traditional homeland. I've spoken to psychologists, but I can't get past the flooding of our homes."

I asked how such an injustice could have occurred?

"You know," a male elder responded. "Greed. Racism. They took our homes away from us, so that they could redirect the water, and build mansions along a peaceful river, while they destroyed our traditional homes."

"We never had a chance," he added. "Even when they were making the negotiations with us, they were building the dam."

The woman cried.

"It's the tradition of our people to give," she continued. "We give all that we have. We share it."

"These people just took," she concluded...

CHAPTER EIGHTEEN

Listening to these events left me at a loss for words. I thought about my family, from whom I'd been disinherited when my grandfather died. Over the past years the relationship with my uncles – who had profited so spectacularly – was proving more difficult, and not less. I had loved them and expected them to be fair trustees. They were not.

"In our culture we talk about taking 'Walking the Good Road,'" the female elder continued. "Others call it, 'The Red Road.' It's the road to balance and harmony. And it doesn't have to be a 'Narrow road.' Just the right road.

"Being Indian is mainly in your heart. It's a way of walking with the earth, instead of upon it. A lot of the history books talk about us Indians in the past tense, but we don't plan on going anywhere. We have lost so much, but the thing that holds us together is that we all belong to and are protectors of the earth; that's the reason for us being here. The Earth is not a resource; she is our mother."

"Still, it's hard for me to accept what's happened here," she concluded.

"But you have to try to come to terms with it," Frank said. "Or else you'll forever be stuck..."

CHAPTER NINETEEN

"Most tribes are affected by historical trauma," Frank began. "And most tribes are affected by oppression. And the recycling of the genocide of our people is still going on.

"And our people are right-brain thinkers. So, you need to get away from IQ back to emotional intelligence and spiritual intelligence. You have to realize that Western therapy is limited. And in order to heal the right brain thinker, you have to go outside the box.

"Here's the deal – right and wrong, good and bad, does not exist. And your thoughts are real powerful. The problem is, we don't see the problem – because we're disconnected. We're fractionated. We're all separated. And that's how we can hurt each other.

"It's because of self-hatred that we can hate each other: What people have done to others, they already done to themselves, or had done to them. Because of that, there's disconnection. But once you start making a shift in perception, people can see themselves, and what they realize is that we're all connected. And then you can treat people the way you would like to be treated.

"So, now, on the left side of some paper, I want you to write the word NOWHERE. Then, I want you to connect with your imagination, and look at the word NOWHERE. I want you to stretch the letters N and O and the W, so now you have, NOW HERE.

"Now, on the right-hand side, I want you to put that. Then, under NOW HERE, I want you to write the word SPIRIT. Underneath spirit, I want you to put the word KNOWING. Under knowing, I want you to put ACCEPTANCE. Under that, LOVE. Under the word, love, I want you to put FAITH. Under faith, I want you to put HOPE. Now, way at the bottom, I want you to put a quote from Rumi – 'There is a field, a place, beyond rightness and wrongness. I will be waiting for you there.' And sign it, 'Spirit.'

"Now when you train your left brain - when you train to see things only one way – 'Believe', 'Logic', 'Skeptic', 'Right and wrong', 'Good and bad.' That's all you're going to see.

"But if you start shifting your perception - start shifting you're thinking. You're not only seeing, 'nowhere', but you're saying, 'Now here.' You move your thought processes back to your right brain. When you know that you're a spirit having a human experience. And you know it. And accept there is an answer to all your problems. Then, there's a spiritual solution to everything. And what follows is love, faith and hope.

"If you stay stuck over at your left brain, logic is real important. Belief is not the same as knowing. And belief is shaped and formed by your environment, and your social conditioning. And underneath, skepticism is connected to unresolved issues. And then with right and wrong, you become a fault finder. And then good and bad, you totally and completely start to get contracted. Can you start to see the different thought processes?… Then, read way at the bottom."

There is a field, a place beyond rightness and wrongness, I will be waiting for you there. Spirit.

"And all our native people and their ceremonies have been affected by historical trauma. By introducing the left-brain philosophy, there's a downward spiral in their language, always fixating on the negative. But over on the right, that shift in perception to 'love, faith, hope' (with that upward spiral of language), there's a resurrection, where we're not stuck in crucifixion; where there is no problem - only opportunity; where things happen for you – not to you.

"And a lot of Indian people are still stuck in trauma, and having been victim. And I once heard that when you have a setback, then you always want to go back, but a go back is not a comeback. So you're stuck in the setback. And the trauma. And you're trying to solve a problem with the same mindset that created it. Doing the same thing over and over again, expecting a different result. It doesn't work. It's called insanity.

"But when you shift your perception, really shift your thinking, there's a transformation that happens in the mind – that right side of the brain, where there's self-evaluation, self-renewal. It all comes down to a renewal of the mind. And once that happens, you start to see things that were not there before - like faith, love, and hope. There's a deep spiritual knowing and realization that there is a Creator - a power greater than ourselves. Nothing happens by mistake. We're at where were supposed to be. Everything is an opportunity to learn, grow and heal…"

"Remember, everything that you went through," he concluded, "all of your life experiences and disappointments – if you had not been through any of that, this exercise that we just done, it might have not meant nothing to you. You would have still been seeing things through nowhere…"

CHAPTER TWENTY

Frank gathered the Runners into the vans and buses to continue their trek; I told him that it was time for us to go our separate ways, and April and I wouldn't be following them this time.

"What will you do now, Dr. Mike?" Frank asked.

I told Frank I was going to the VA.

"I know," he responded. "But what will you do after that? Where will you take what you've experienced with us?"

I thought of the daughters of Chief Red Cloud, then turned to Frank and stared him in the eye.

"I'm going to learn their ways," I said. "And I'll take what I learn, and whatever the Indian Health Service doesn't have that the VA does, I'll endeavor to bring it to the IHS, so to better serve native peoples."

"That's it!" he responded, spiritedly. "That's it! I know that you're on a spiritual quest. And you still have some ways to go. And those times when you hit walls – and you got so frustrated and were so depressed – those were pivot points of redirection, and reset to a solution in spirit, and other opportunities.

"I knew that you're on a spirit quest when I first met you over there and you were really deeply involved and you believed in what you were doing. And I know that since that time till now, you still believe and you're still deeply involved. Just in another direction for reform.

"My advice – what comes up for me – is you can't solve a problem with the same mindset that created it. And you can't deal with ego from ego when the lights have gone out.

"And I know that it takes spirits like you to create that movement. Those who are ordained and blessed to be able to do what you do.

"You're awakening from an amnesia. And the reform that you're talking about, I think is part of the awakening from the spiritual amnesia. Just don't get ahead of yourself. Be fearless and courageous and, well, take care of yourself. April will be right there beside you – and you beside her."

"And remember," he concluded. "Don't just be a Dreamer, be a Dreamkeeper. Don't speak of it, live it. You are certainly sharing a dream worthy of keeping..."

EPILOGUE

Shortly after starting work at the VA, I became aware of a program called "Compensated Work Therapy" that provided jobs and training to unemployed Veterans and was exceedingly beneficial to the homeless Veteran patients I was charged with serving. When I considered how helpful a program like this could be to native peoples on the Reservations (where unemployment was as high as 90%), I reached back to IHS Headquarters and proposed the "Dreamkeepers Program", a VA-styled Compensated Work Therapy programs would be established to serve native peoples, starting with Native Veterans and then moving to encompass all members of the tribe. Ultimately, the program exceeded my expectations, providing a path for establishing a Compensated Work Therapy program not only at every Reservation in the country, but also every Urban Indian Health Center.

Some ten years later, as I was organizing and reviewing the initiatives I'd overseen during my tenure as Director of Homeless Primary Care, I regarded the Dreamkeepers program as the most significant and important of those initiatives. When I shared this with my wife, she looked at me, approvingly.

"So, something good came out of something bad," she said...

ABOUT THE AUTHOR

Michael Yanuck MD PhD is a physician-scientist
whose groundbreaking research at the National Institutes of
Health was the basis for a FDA-approved vaccine for cancer.
Following a traumatic leg injury he returned to medicine. Intent on
helping those most in need, he enlisted in the National Health
Service Corps, worked in urban and rural health centers throughout
the country, then served native peoples in the Indian Health Service.
After three years in the field, he was selected Deputy Director of the
Office of Clinical & Preventive Services at IHS Headquarters.
Transferring to the VA, he spearheaded the Dreamkeepers Program –
a Compensated Work Therapy (CWT) program to help Native
Veterans acquire meaningful work on Indian Reservations and Urban
Indian Health Centers nationwide, reducing poverty, homelessness,
suicide, alcohol and substance abuse, physical and sexual abuse,
crime, arrests, incarceration, ER visits, hospitalization
(medical and psychiatric), and improving the health
and wellbeing of native peoples.

www.ingramcontent.com/pod-product-compliance
Lightning Source LLC
Chambersburg PA
CBHW071939020426
42331CB00010B/2932